EARLIER AMERICAN MUSIC

EDITED BY H. WILEY HITCHCOCK

for the *Music Library Association*

4

SYMPHONY NO. 2

BY GEORGE W. CHADWICK

GEORGE W. CHADWICK

SYMPHONY NO. 2
(Op. 21)

NEW INTRODUCTION BY H. WILEY HITCHCOCK

Director, Institute for Studies in American Music,
Brooklyn College, CUNY

DA CAPO PRESS • NEW YORK • 1972

This Da Capo Press edition of *Symphony No. 2* by
George W. Chadwick is an unabridged republication of
the first edition published in Boston in 1888. It is
reprinted with permission from a copy of that edition
in the collection of the University of Illinois Library.

Library of Congress Catalog Card Number 71-170930

ISBN 0-306-77304-X

Published by Da Capo Press, Inc.
A Subsidiary of Plenum Publishing Corporation
227 West 17th Street, New York, New York 10011

EDITOR'S FOREWORD

American musical culture, from Colonial and Federal Era days on, has been reflected in an astonishing production of printed music of all kinds: by 1820, for instance, more than fifteen thousand musical publications had issued from American presses. Fads, fashions, and tastes have changed so rapidly in our history, however, that comparatively little earlier American music has remained in print. On the other hand, the past few decades have seen an explosion of interest in earlier American culture, including earlier American music. College and university courses in American civilization and American music have proliferated; recording companies have found a surprising response to earlier American composers and their music; a wave of interest in folk and popular music of past eras has opened up byways of musical experience unimagined only a short time ago.

It seems an opportune moment, therefore, to make available for study and enjoyment — and as an aid to furthering performance of earlier American music — works of significance that exist today only in a few scattered copies of publications long out of print, and works that may be well known only in later editions or arrangements having little relationship to the original compositions.

Earlier American Music is planned around several types of musical scores to be reprinted from early editions of the eighteenth, nineteenth, and early twentieth centuries. The categories are as follows:

> Songs and other solo vocal music
> Choral music and part-songs
> Solo keyboard music
> Chamber music
> Orchestral music and concertos
> Dance music and marches for band
> Theater music

The idea of *Earlier American Music* originated in a paper read before the Music Library Association in February, 1968, and published under the title "A Monumenta Americana?" in the Association's journal, *Notes* (September, 1968). It seems most appropriate, therefore, for the Music Library Association to sponsor this series. We hope *Earlier American Music* will stimulate further study and performance of musical Americana.

H. Wiley Hitchcock

INTRODUCTION

Like almost all the composers who have been called as a group "The Second New England School" and who dominated American art-music from about 1880 to 1920, George Whitefield Chadwick (1854–1931) took his main musical studies in Germany. This was not surprising since under the sway of Romanticism, which had made its greatest impact through Germanic music and musicians, the main centers of mid-nineteenth-century musical thought were considered to be Berlin, Leipzig, Munich, and Vienna; and the ultimate in fine-art music was considered to be German. It was only natural, then, that young, aspiring American musicians, especially composers like Chadwick, were packed off to Germany, as to a finishing school, to acquire final polish.

One significant result of this pattern of training was the rejection by such men of both the American musical past, dominated as it had been by "unscientific" taste and British backgrounds, and the American musical present—that of revival hymnody, minstrel-show tunes, and other folkish and popular music. The late nineteenth-century New Englanders' music was thoroughly Germanized. Only in the twentieth century would American music, infused with strains from Russian and French music and from the great reservoir of its own native tradition, broaden its base and enlarge its expression.

In this light, some of Chadwick's work has a special interest, for he was one of the first to reveal a sympathy for American vernacular-tradition music and to accept American folkish and popular materials as worthy sources for his art-music. He was not as naturally and unabashedly able to do so as Charles Ives, nor did he make a fetish out of nativism in the manner of Arthur Farwell or Henry Gilbert. But unlike John Knowles Paine and Horatio Parker, among others, he was not wholly isolated from the American vernacular-music tradition—indeed, he actually anticipated Ives and Farwell, although in slight, subtle, and unself-proclaiming ways.

We hear this side of Chadwick in his Symphony No. 2. One might imagine that the principal theme of its first movement had been inspired by the "Goin' home" motif from Dvorak's "New World" Symphony, or that that of the second movement had followed Dvorak's recommendation, in a much-discussed and very influential article in *Harper's*, that American composers turn to Negro melodies, "the folk songs of America." But the "New World" Symphony was a work of 1893 and the *Harper's* article appeared in 1895, while Chadwick's Second dates from 1886.

Apart from its manifest debt to some inflections of American folk music, the Symphony No. 2 is a solid, craftsmanly, post-Romantic symphony in the standard four-movement pattern, owing much to Schumann and Mendelssohn, and perhaps a bit to Brahms as well. It well merits revival, not just as a work of historical interest but as a competent and enjoyable work of art.

H. W. H.

MEINEM LEBENSFREUNDE

A. T. Scott.

SYMPHONY

Nº 2.

(IN B FLAT)

BY

G.W. CHADWICK.

Op. 21.

BOSTON:
ARTHUR P. SCHMIDT & Cº,
13 and 15 West Street.

Meinem Lebensfreunde
A. T. Scott.

SYMPHONY II.
I.

G. W. Chadwick, Op. 21.

6

à 2.
ff
ff
ff
à 2.
ff
ff marcato
ff marcato
ff marcato
ff
ff
8
ff
ff
ff
ff
ff

57

II.

76

84

III.

Largo e maestoso. ($\quad$ = 52.)

Allegro non troppo. (♩=120.)

124

Assai con fuoco.

F Allegro con fuoco.

F Allegro con fuoco.

attacca Finale.

IV.

Allegro molto animato. (♩-132.)

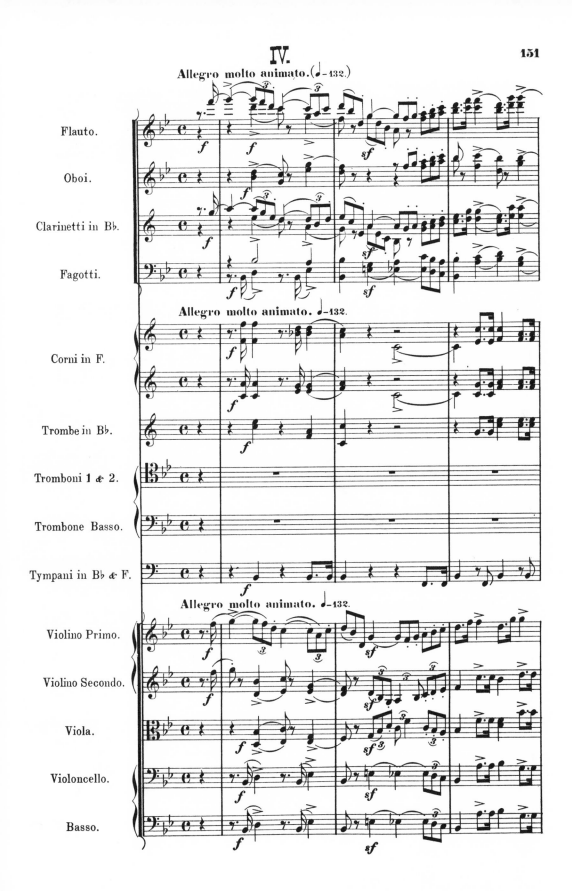

Fine.

Fine.